CULTURE IN ACTION

Staging a Play

Deborah Underwood

Raintree

Chicago, Illinois

www.heinemannraintree.com
Visit our website to find out
more information about
Heinemann-Raintree books.

To order:
☎ Phone 888-454-2279
💻 Visit www.heinemannraintree.com
to browse our catalog and order online.

©2010 Raintree
an imprint of Capstone Global Library, LLC
Chicago, Illinois

Edited by Louise Galpine, Abby Colich, and Laura J. Hensley
Designed by Kimberly Miracle and Betsy Wernert
Original illustrations © Capstone Global Library Ltd.
Illustrated by kja-artists.com
Picture research by Mica Brancic and Kay Altwegg
Production by Alison Parsons
Originated by Dot Gradations Ltd.
Printed in China by Leo Paper Products Ltd

13 12 11 10 09
10 9 8 7 6 5 4 3 2 1

Library of Congress Cataloging-in-Publication Data
Underwood, Deborah.
  Staging a play / Deborah Underwood.
     p. cm. -- (Culture in action)
  Includes bibliographical references and index.
  ISBN 978-1-4109-3396-6 (hc) -- ISBN 978-1-4109-3413-
0 (pb) 1. Theater--Production and direction--Juvenile
literature. I. Title.
  PN2053.U53 2009
  792.02'32--dc22
                              2009000417

Acknowledgments

The author and publishers are grateful to the following for
permission to reproduce copyright material: ©Alamy pp. **9**
(Jim West), **10** (Paul Wood), **18 top** (Keith Morris), **18 bottom**
(Richard Levine), **24** (Jim West), **26** (Chad Ehlers), **27** (The
Photolibrary Wales), **28** (Paul Wood); ©Corbis pp. **4, 5** (LWA-
Dann Tardif), **7 top** (Robbie Jack), **7 bottom** (Robbie Jack), **14**
(Robbie Jack), **20** (Deepeyes Photo/Yann Dejardin), **21** (Kelly-
Mooney Photography), **22** (Ryan Pyle), **23** (Sygma/Micheline
Pelletier), **25** (Lacy Atkins); ©Getty Images pp. **6** (Cate Gillon),
16 (Steve Finn), **29** (Scott Eells); ©JupiterImages p. **8** (Polka
Dot); ©Rex Features p. **17** (FremantleMedia, Ltd./Sally Head
Productions); ©Theatre in the Round Players, Inc. p. **13**.

Icon and banner images supplied by Shutterstock: © Alexander
Lukin, © ornitopter, © Colorlife, and © David S. Rose.

Cover photograph of theatrical tudor woman on stage
with mask reproduced with permission of Getty Imges/
Photographer's Choice/ Colin Anderson.

We would like to thank Nancy Harris, Jackie Murphy, Ken
Cerniglia, and Colleen Rosati for their invaluable help in the
preparation of this book.

Every effort has been made to contact copyright holders of
any material reproduced in this book. Any omissions will be
rectified in subsequent printings if notice is given to
the publisher.

All the Internet addresses (URLs) given in this book were valid
at the time of going to press. However, due to the dynamic
nature of the Internet, some addresses may have changed, or
sites may have changed or ceased to exist since publication.
While the author and publisher regret any inconvenience this
may cause readers, no responsibility for any such changes can
be accepted by either the author or the publisher.

Contents

Some words are printed in bold, **like this**. You can find out what they mean by looking in the glossary on page 30.

Theater Magic

It is Saturday night, and a group of actors is getting ready to put on a play. A man puts on makeup and a long gray wig. He drapes a cape around his shoulders and places a crown on his head. When he is finished, he looks like an old king. Other actors use costumes and makeup to become princesses and dukes.

Behind the stage curtain, a man moves a throne into place. Two women slide a large, upright piece of wood into position at the back of the stage. Gray stones painted on the wood make it look like the inside wall of a castle.

More than just actors

During a play, the audience sees only the actors. But putting on a play requires many other people, too. Someone must choose who plays each **role** and help the actors **rehearse**. Someone must decide what the stage will look like. Someone must make costumes. Together, these people and many others bring a play to life.

A crown and cape turn an actor into a king.

Showtime

When it is time for the play to begin, the sound of trumpets fills the theater. The red velvet curtain opens and an old king hobbles onstage. The audience watches eagerly as the actors tell the king's story.

When the show is over, the audience claps. The actors come back onstage to take their bows. The actor who played the king stands up straight. He walks quickly, no longer bent and frail. Like the other actors, he has become himself again.

A play may be performed in a school gym or in a fancy theater.

What Is a Production?

A person who writes a play is called a **playwright**. After a play is written, it may be chosen by a theater. A team of people then works to bring the play to life on a stage. A **director** leads this team.

The director

The director of a play does many jobs. He or she chooses the actors and helps them **rehearse**. The director works with the people in charge of the show's costumes, scenery, and lights. Most importantly, the director has an overall plan for what the show should be like. Everyone else helps to turn the director's vision into reality.

William Shakespeare

One of the most famous playwrights of all time was also an actor. William Shakespeare lived in England from around 1564 to 1616. He wrote more than three dozen plays, including *Hamlet* and *A Midsummer Night's Dream*. His plays are still performed all over the world.

The director leads the team of people who work on a play.

A traditional production

Two directors may have different visions for the same play. For example, one director might set Shakespeare's *Hamlet* in long-ago Denmark, as Shakespeare intended. (See box at left for more about Shakespeare.) Actors might wear costumes appropriate for that time and place. This type of play would be a traditional **production** (see photo at top right).

This is a traditional production of *Hamlet*.

A modern production

Another director might set *Hamlet* in a different time and place, such as a modern-day city. A new setting makes people look at a play in a new way. In a modern production, Shakespeare's characters might wear tuxedos and evening gowns (see photo at bottom right).

This is a modern production of *Hamlet*.

The actors in traditional and modern productions say exactly the same lines. But the shows may seem very different because of each director's vision for the play. Each production of a play is different. This is one of the things that makes theater exciting.

Actors and Rehearsals

One of the **director's** most important jobs is to **cast** the play. Often many actors want to play the same part in a show. Directors usually hold **auditions**, or tryouts, to help them decide who should play each **role**.

Choosing the actors

During an audition, actors may read lines from the play's **script**. They may perform **monologues** they have prepared. A monologue is a short piece for one actor. If the play is a musical, actors may sing and dance for the director, too.

After the director sees all the auditions, he or she decides who gets which part. The director may cast some people as understudies. An understudy learns a role in case an actor gets sick.

During some auditions, the actors sing for a director.

During early rehearsals, actors read from their scripts.

Rehearsing the show

Once the actors have been cast, rehearsals begin. The director talks with the actors about his or her vision for the play. The director also helps the actors understand the characters they will play. At first, the actors read their lines from the script. Over time, they memorize their lines.

Other people may help actors with their parts. If actors need to speak with accents, a coach may teach them how. A voice teacher or music coach may work with actors who need to sing in a show.

All actors need to **rehearse** before a show.

Playing a part

To play a role well, an actor must show the audience what his or her character is feeling. Actors have tools to help them do this. Some actors use a tool called sense memory.

Sense memory

An actor who plays a character who is sad may think of a time when he or she was sad in real life. For instance, the actor may think about when a friend moved away. The actor may remember how he or she behaved when sad. He or she may have walked more slowly, spoken in a lower tone of voice, or stared off into space. These memories help the actor to play the part of the sad character.

Use your sense memories

This exercise will help you use sense memories the way that actors do.

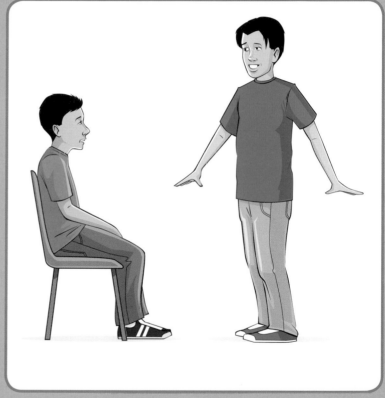

Steps to follow:

1. Think about something that made you feel happy. How did happiness make your body feel? Did you smile? Did you bounce up and down on your toes? Did you talk more quickly? Remember what happiness felt like, then say this line out loud: "You won't believe what happened to me today."

2. Now think about something that made you feel sad. Remember how that felt, then read the line again.

3. Think about something that made you feel angry. Remember that feeling, then read the line a third time.

Try doing this in front of a friend. See if your friend can tell what feeling you are expressing. You can also try this with other feelings, such as boredom or fright. Try thinking of different lines you can say to express these different emotions.

Moving onstage

Where and how actors move while they are onstage is called **blocking**. Directors create blocking for a play. They use a special language to describe the parts of the stage. In the past, stages were tilted forward to help the audience see. The part of the stage nearest an audience is still called "downstage" because of this. The area farthest from the audience is "upstage." "Stage right" means the actors' right when they are facing the audience, and "stage left" means the actors' left (see diagram below).

A director uses blocking to help an audience understand the story and characters better. If an actor stomps across the stage and slams a door, it is easy to see that the character is angry. If two characters are in love, the director might have the actors sit close together.

This diagram shows the different areas of a stage.

AUDIENCE		
downstage left	downstage center	downstage right
left center	center	right center
upstage left	upstage center	upstage right

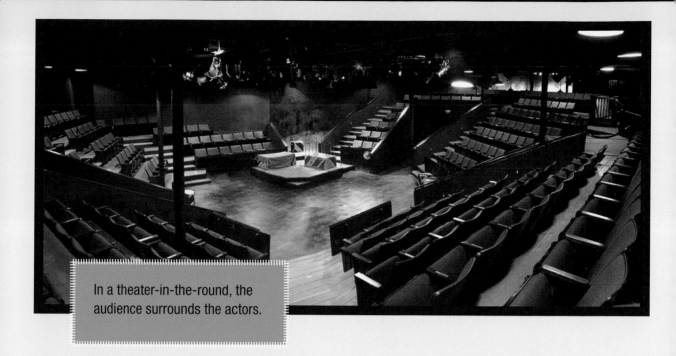

In a theater-in-the-round, the audience surrounds the actors.

Some theaters have special blocking needs. In a theater-in-the-round, the audience surrounds the actors in a circle. The director must make sure that no one in the audience sees only the actors' backs.

In a musical play, actors may dance. A **choreographer** makes up the dances and teaches them to the actors.

Staging fights

During some plays, characters fight with swords or their fists. A fight choreographer plans out these fights and helps the actors learn the moves. The actors practice slowly at first, so they will not get hurt when they perform the fight at normal speed. They practice the fight in slow motion before every show. This keeps the actors safe.

Sets and Props

The scenery, furniture, and other items onstage during a **scene** are called the **set**. A set can make a stage look like anything from a forest to a living room. There may be many set changes between scenes.

A **set designer** decides how a stage should look. The designer chooses colors and shapes for the sets that match the mood of the play. A scary play, for example, would probably have a dark set.

Backdrops

Sets often use backdrops. A backdrop is a large piece of wood or fabric with a picture of a setting painted on it. A backdrop is lowered or pulled into place at the back of the stage before a scene.

First, the set designer draws sketches. Then he or she makes a model of each set to show the **director**. Carpenters and painters may help to build the final sets.

A set helps an audience understand where a play is taking place.

Build a set model

You can make your own set model out of a shoebox and paper.

Steps to follow:

1. Draw a set design for a scene from a story you know. For instance, you could draw a design for the scene where Little Red Riding Hood first meets the wolf.

2. Make a set model based on your design. Cut one of the long sides off a shoebox. Use stiff paper, tape, crayons, or other art supplies to make the set.

3. Draw and cut out characters and place them in your model.

4. Display your model for others to see.

Props

Objects used by actors during a play are called theatrical properties, or **props**. A play might have a scene in which a family eats dinner. This scene would require props such as dishes, napkins, and silverware.

A hand prop is a small prop that an actor handles, such as a cell phone or sword. Hand props are kept backstage on a prop table. That way the actors can always find the props they need for each scene.

An actor may use a prop such as this sword during a show.

During a show, props are kept on a prop table so the actors can easily find them.

The prop master

A person called a prop master is often in charge of finding props. The prop master may need to do research. He or she may need to find out what kind of television would have been found in a 1960s home, or what kind of pen a writer in 1770 would have used.

A play may have many sets, each with different props. For some shows, actors help to prepare the set for each scene. For others, people called **stagehands** move sets and large props into place before the show. Stagehands also go onstage between scenes to change the sets.

Staged readings

Some performances do not use sets or props at all. In a staged reading, the actors read from **scripts**. They do not wear costumes. Staged readings are sometimes done when a **playwright** is working on a new play. The playwright may make changes to the play, depending on how the reading goes.

Light and Sound

Lighting can change a stage into a bright meadow or a spooky forest. A **lighting designer** decides how a stage should be lit. Bright lights called spotlights may follow actors as they move onstage. Colored sheets called gels change a light's color. Cutouts in front of a spotlight make shadows onstage.

Different lights help a lighting designer create different effects.

A **sound designer** plans a show's sounds. For instance, a phone may need to ring during a play. The sound designer makes sure that everyone in the audience can hear the actors and other sounds during the show.

Music can help create a play's mood. For instance, a play set in the 1940s might have music from that time playing between **scenes**. An orchestra may play during a musical. The orchestra usually sits in an orchestra pit, a low area in front of or below the stage.

A sound designer and lighting designer might work together to create effects such as a thunderstorm. Pounding on a large sheet of metal makes the sound of thunder. A light flashing on and off can look like lightning.

The people who operate the sounds and lights often sit behind the audience. From there they can watch the show and make sure everything happens at the right time.

The sound board controls the sounds used in a play.

Mood music

Try matching music with different moods!

Steps to follow:

1. Listen to several songs, and choose one that you could use for a scene set in a teenager's room this year.

2. Choose music that you could use for a scary scene.

3. Listen to one of your favorite songs. What type of scene might match its mood? Pretend you are a sound designer and describe this scene.

Costumes and Makeup

An audience can learn a lot about a play's characters from the actors' costumes and makeup. Imagine an actor walked on stage wearing a shimmering gown, wings, and glittery makeup. The audience would probably guess that the character is a fairy.

An actor might wear a ragged shirt and have smudges of dirt on his face. The audience would think that character does not have much money. Costumes and makeup help actors feel more like their characters.

Actors in *The Lion King* become animals with the help of costumes.

Julie Taymor

U.S. director Julie Taymor directed the stage version of Disney's *The Lion King*. She won awards both for directing and for the costumes she designed. Costumes that were part puppet changed the actors into African animals.

Costume designers

A **costume designer** works with the **director** to decide what the actors should wear. Like other designers, costume designers do research. They must find out what people wore during the time the play takes place. They may look through books that show clothes from many periods of history. They consider both when and where the play is set. A play that is set in China will need different costumes than one set in England, for example.

A costume designer may find or make the costumes alone. Or the designer may lead a team of people who buy, cut, and sew fabric to create the costumes, then make sure they fit the actors correctly.

Professional theaters have costume shops where they keep costumes after a show is over. These costumes—or parts of them—may be used again for other shows.

After costumes are designed, they must be sewn and fitted to the actors.

Makeup designers

If you see actors close-up right after a play, you might notice they look different than they did onstage. Most likely, they will be wearing heavy makeup that you might not have noticed during the performance. Actors often wear a thick makeup called pancake makeup all over their faces. They may also put color on their eyelids, cheeks, and lips.

Makeup designers decide what makeup will be used for performances. Makeup can help change actors into different people. Actors can use makeup to make themselves look older or younger. For example, lines drawn on the face with a dark makeup pencil look like wrinkles onstage. Makeup can even make actors look like animals (see box at right)!

Even an actor whose character should look normal must wear makeup onstage. Stage lights are very strong. Without makeup, an actor would look pale and washed-out. Actors often put on their own stage makeup. If the makeup is complicated, a makeup artist may help them.

Wig designers

Some shows require fancy hairstyles. Actors may need to wear wigs, fake beards, or fake mustaches. A wig designer may design the hairstyles. Others in the wig department help actors put the hairpieces on and take them off.

Cats

The musical *Cats* by British composer Andrew Lloyd Webber tells the story of a group of human-like cats. The show is based on a book of poems by T. S. Eliot. The musical ran for 21 years in London. This adds up to nearly 9,000 performances! *Cats* has been performed in more than 20 countries.

Makeup helps turn these actors into cats.

Final Rehearsals

It may take weeks, or even months, to prepare a play. While **sets** are built and costumes are sewn, the actors keep **rehearsing**. Early on, they may practice in a normal room. As the first performance nears, they begin to rehearse in the theater.

The **stage manager** goes to all the rehearsals. He or she keeps a special copy of the **script** called the prompt book. The stage manager writes down all the **blocking** in this book. During performances, the stage manager "calls" the show. This means he or she tells people when to change the lights, sounds, and sets. All these changes are written down in the prompt book.

During a performance, the stage manager makes sure the play runs smoothly.

Actors get used to wearing their costumes during dress rehearsals.

Dress rehearsals begin when the show is **opening** in just a few days. During dress rehearsals, all the parts of the show come together for the first time. The actors wear costumes and makeup. Sets and **props** are in place. The lighting people run the lights, and the sound people run the sound.

The goal of the dress rehearsal is to catch any problems before the show opens. Dress rehearsals also help actors get used to moving in their costumes and wearing their makeup.

Other jobs

There are many other people who help put on a play. The **house manager** makes sure the theater is in good condition. He or she may hire ticket sellers and the ushers who show people to their seats. Publicity people may make posters and put out advertisements to tell people about the play.

Opening Night

The first time a play is officially performed for the public is called the **opening**. Opening night is an exciting time for everyone involved in the play. All the pieces of the play come together just as in the **dress rehearsal**. But one very important piece is added: the audience.

Break a leg!

You may hear people say, "Break a leg" to actors before a show. They don't really want the actors to hurt themselves! Some actors think hearing "good luck" is actually unlucky. So people tell actors to "break a leg" instead.

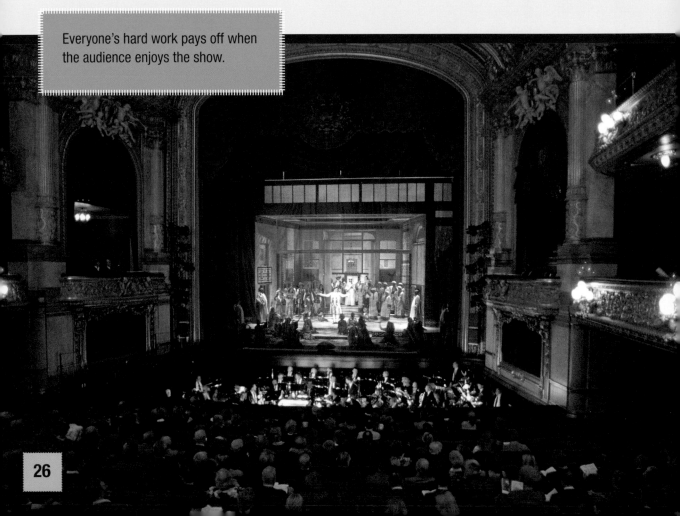

Everyone's hard work pays off when the audience enjoys the show.

After the show

After the show, the actors go onstage to take a curtain call, or bow, as the audience applauds. Then they go backstage to take off their makeup and hang up their costumes. The **stagehands** get the stage ready for the next performance. Finally, everyone leaves the theater—until the next night, when they may do it all again.

If the play is a school play or a play in a small town, there may be only one performance. **Professional** theater companies may perform a show eight times in one week! Popular shows in big cities can run for years.

After a play opens, the **stage manager** makes sure the play stays the way the **director** wanted. The director may move on to a job at another theater. There he or she begins rehearsals for another play, starting the cycle all over again.

After a performance, the actors take a curtain call.

A Few Famous Playwrights and Plays

William Shakespeare

William Shakespeare is one of the most famous **playwrights** of all time. He lived in England from around 1564 to 1616. Shakespeare was an actor as well as a playwright. He wrote at least 37 plays, as well as many poems. In the play *Romeo and Juliet*, two young people fall in love, even though their families are enemies. They decide to run away together, with unhappy results.

J. M. Barrie

J. M. Barrie was a Scottish writer. He lived from 1860 to 1937. He attended college in Scotland, then moved in 1885 to London. There he wrote many novels as well as plays. His most famous play is *Peter Pan*, which was first performed in 1904. It tells the story of Peter Pan, a boy who refuses to grow up, and the three children with whom he shares his adventures in Neverland.

In J. M. Barrie's play *Peter Pan*, Peter must battle the evil Captain Hook.

Thornton Wilder

Thornton Wilder was a U.S. playwright and novelist. He lived from 1897 to 1975. The popular musical *Hello Dolly!* was based on Wilder's play *The Matchmaker*. Wilder's most famous play, *Our Town*, is about the lives of the people in an imaginary town called Grover's Corners. In 1938 *Our Town* won the Pulitzer Prize for Drama, an important award for an outstanding U.S. play.

Lorraine Hansberry

Lorraine Hansberry was a U.S. writer who lived from 1930 to 1965. Born in Chicago, she moved to New York City in 1950. Her play *A Raisin in the Sun* is about the challenges of an African-American family living in Chicago. It was the first play by a black woman to be produced on Broadway. (Broadway is an area of New York City where major plays and musicals are performed.) The New York Drama Critics' Circle named *A Raisin in the Sun* the best U.S. play of 1959.

Rapper and actor Sean "Diddy" Combs has starred in both stage and made-for-television **productions** of *A Raisin in the Sun*. Here, he is shown onstage holding a T-shirt with a photograph of Lorraine Hansberry.

Glossary

audition tryout for a play or show. During an audition, actors read lines from the play.

blocking movements actors make onstage. Blocking helps an audience understand what is happening in a play.

cast assign roles in a play. A director casts the actors in a play.

choreographer person who plans the dances in a musical. A choreographer teaches actors the dance moves in a show.

costume designer person who plans the clothes actors wear for a play. A costume designer might select or make the actors' costumes.

director leader of the team that puts on a play. A director plans what a play will be like.

dress rehearsal full run-through of a play with lights, costumes, and makeup. Dress rehearsals begin when a show is opening in just a few days.

house manager person who makes sure the theater runs smoothly. A house manager may hire ticket sellers and ushers.

lighting designer person who plans a play's lighting. A lighting designer decides how a stage should be lit during a performance.

makeup designer person who plans the makeup for a play. A makeup designer may use makeup to make a person look older, for example.

monologue piece that an actor can act out alone. During an audition, an actor may perform a monologue.

opening first performance of a show. Opening night is an exciting time for everyone involved in a play.

playwright person who writes a play. One of the most famous playwrights of all time was William Shakespeare.

production play or show that is performed in a theater for an audience. Each production of a play is different.

professional related to a career or job for which workers are paid. Professional theater companies may perform eight times each week.

prop object onstage that an actor handles. A hand prop is a small prop, such as a cell phone or sword.

rehearse practice. Actors sometimes rehearse a play for weeks before an audience sees it.

role part in a play. To play a role well, an actor must show the audience what his or her character is feeling.

scene section of a play that happens in one setting at one time. Different scenes may be set in different places.

script written copy of a play. Until they have memorized their lines, actors read their parts from a script.

set scenery and furniture that is onstage during a scene. A set helps an audience understand where a play is taking place.

set designer person who plans a play's scenery. Set designers use models to help them decide how a set should look.

sound designer person who plans a play's sound. The sound designer makes sure that everyone in the audience can hear the actors.

stagehand person who helps move sets and props on and off the stage. Stagehands go onstage between scenes to change the sets.

stage manager person who helps the director and makes sure the show runs smoothly. The stage manager tells people when to change the lights, sounds, and sets during a performance.

Find Out More

Books

Elgin, Kathy. *Theater and Entertainment* (*Changing Times*). Mankato, Minn.: Compass Point, 2005.

Friedman, Lise. *Break a Leg! The Kid's Guide to Acting and Stagecraft*. New York: Workman, 2002.

Nesbit, Edith. *The Children's Shakespeare*. Chicago: Academy Chicago, 2000.

Schumacher, Thomas, with Jeff Kurtti. *How Does the Show Go On?: An Introduction to the Theater*. New York: Disney, 2007.

Websites

Children's Creative Theater Guide
http://library.thinkquest.org/5291/

Zoom Playhouse
http://pbskids.org/zoom/activities/playhouse/

Index